T0150677

Death and Exes

DEATH AND EXES
SARAH BRIDGINS

THE **BLACK SPRING**
PRESS GROUP

First published in 2022
Eyewear Publishing Ltd, an imprint of The Black Spring Press Group
Grantully Road, Maida Vale, London w9
United Kingdom

Typesetting User Design, Illustration and Typesetting, UK
Cover art Kendra Allenby

The publisher has followed American spelling and grammar at the request of the poet

ISBN-13 978-1-915406-19-4

CONTENTS

ENDORSEMENTS

Lisa Marie Basile, author of *City Witchery*:

"Sarah Bridgins' work is made of both bite and beauty. At times, it hurts to read, begs you to peer deep into the waters of truth. *All my apertures are open*, Bridgins writes – and, reader, you can feel it. They are. What looks back at you from the depths is your own heart. Good poetry does that – forces you to face yourself through someone else's horror. And it forces you to find hope, through someone else's light.

This is a poetry of small, sharp details – humor that teeters on oblivion which inches toward divinity. Bridgins manages to carry and translate so much. *I sat across from you, my stomach full of flesh, drinking the ashes of the dead*, she writes. In her poetry, you can taste the tears and the wine, and it's dizzying."

Natalie Eilbert, author of *Overland*:

"Kevin Costner, Whitney Houston, Meg Ryan, Dolly Parton, a medicated princess defiantly alive: the characters of grief swirl with kaleidoscopic whim in Sarah Bridgins' debut poetry collection, *Death and Exes*. The collisions of death in Bridgins' life deliver readers through a reluctant kind of survival, a contradiction of terms. There's a sorrow to this book that looks directly at itself, as when the broken-hearted speaker compares herself with severed human parts in the Mütter Museum that exist in a future despite themselves. Bridgins' is a world fraught with loss but also attitude. Honest, sad, unexpectedly sassy, *Death and Exes* examines the junky inheritance of continuing to live – and to love – at the end of the world."

Wren Hanks, author of *Lily-livered*:

"*Death and Exes* is a sharp, sexy meditation on the trash and glitter of grief – the 'satisfying portion' of scorched Stouffer's Mac, impulse-buy cocktail dresses and stuffed animals as support groups, the last gag gift you ever gave your dad. Bridgins' poems brazenly embrace the void and fill it with late-night 7–11; I have never wanted so badly to mourn the bad, forgettable men of my life while reaching for a Cherry Coke slushee.

'Take all the comfort you can / from useless things,' the speaker advises in 'Theory of Everything,' planning for a loft filled with 'purebred cats' in a post-grief future where 'nothing will ever be okay again.' In 'Sea of Crises,' Bridgins responds to our stone-cold tradition of timestamping sadness by offering the most American alternative: transfer the love you can't keep into an object so beautiful you'll feel like you've already won."

Rachel Lyon, author of *Self-Portrait with Boy*:

"Thrumming with frank grief, sharp humor, and coruscating desire, in the candidly erotic tradition of Sharon Olds, Sarah Bridgins' poems will gut you with a rhinestone cake knife and leave you for dead."

The Sexton Poetry Prize, a note from Judge Lloyd Schwartz

"What a pleasure it has been reading the submissions for Eyewear's annual Sexton Prize, this year. Among the twelve finalists, any one of the manuscripts could have made a plausible winner. These entries were all intelligent, ambitious, serious, formally intriguing, often witty, and often quite moving.

But two remarkable manuscripts distinctly stood out for me: Ross White's *Charm Offensive* and Sarah Bridgins' *Death and Exes*.

And after reading and re-reading them many times, I couldn't choose one over the other. Each one deserves publication and each one deserves first prize.

Perhaps, as Ross White says in the title of his introductory poem, "I Like Too Many Things." But in both cases, while these books are very different from one another, what they had in common was a truly individual and convincing voice.

Every word seemed personal and deeply felt, as if both of these poets urgently needed to tell me what they were thinking. Not a single poem in either of these collections ended where I expected it to—as if each writer was engaged in the process of discovering in the course of a poem what it was they each had to say, not just merely producing good poems that sounded like other good poems. And both of these poets have their own quirkily humorous and ironic view of the world, and of themselves.

I admired them for seeming to take their poems more seriously than they took themselves. Nothing in either of these books feels either effortful or over-simplified, or predictable.

Elizabeth Bishop once wrote that the poetry she liked best shared the qualities of "accuracy, spontaneity, mystery." I found those qualities in both of these collections, and I am very pleased to have both Ross White and Sarah Bridgins share first prize.

My congratulations."

For Justin

SO EMOTIONAL

I had the good fortune of Whitney Houston dying
the week before my mother did.
The soundtrack to my first trip to the hospital
was songs I sang in fourth grade at lunch,
"So Emotional," "I Wanna Dance With Somebody,"
"I Will Always Love You."

My mom hated Whitney Houston's version of
"I Will Always Love You."
She said that wasn't singing, it was shouting.

I still prefer Dolly Parton's version.

I think only substance abusers fall asleep in the bathtub.

When I was little my dad used to warn me
to be careful in the bathtub because a few times
my mom almost drowned.

Today I watched Kevin Costner's eulogy for Whitney Houston.
When he said the line about being
"escorted by an army of angels to your heavenly father,"
I became very emotional.
I was going to make my boyfriend watch it,
but then I got embarrassed at being moved
by Kevin Costner.

Kevin Costner said Whitney Houston made
"God wonder how He created something so perfect."

My mother was beautiful.

She was not perfect.

I guess neither was Whitney Houston.

WHEN LOVE GOES WRONG

I want to marry for money
instead of attention.
I want to count the things I care about.

I am tired of men who put
their heads on my chest,
tell me my heart is beating their name,
then leave me for caring too much.

If someone tells you that being
a showgirl will make you more attractive
they're lying. I've tried it.
The glitter prevents intimacy,
gets into everything and never
comes off, spreads like an infection.

It's okay.
When I fall in the pool
with all my clothes on it will be
because an Olympic diver pushed me.
In court I'll sing show tunes, wear fishnets.
My wedding ring will be
a diamond tiara.

MAJOR DELUSIONS

"In fact, the people who accurately predict the likelihood of coming events tend to be mildly depressed. The rest of us systematically fail when interpreting the crystal ball."
  —Tali Sharot, *The New York Times*

I had a strawberry Poptart for breakfast,
and I'm holding you responsible.

Is Red #40 an anti-depressant?

"I still think I'm 16," you said in the middle of a fight.
"I'm always shocked that I can buy airplane tickets."

16: While you were doing X and having threesomes
I was going out to dinner with my dad
on Friday nights, hoping to find a toothpick
in my sandwich so they would give me free dessert.

"Which plant are you watering?
Your negative plant or your positive plant?"
asked the drag queen teaching
my self-confidence workshop.

My negative plant eats goldfish,
my positive plant is digging its own grave.

I SHOULDN'T BE ALIVE

At the end I became obsessed with disasters:
specials on Katrina, articles
about parents who left their kids in cars,
then came back hours later to find
their small bodies baked, insides a stew.
"How can you watch this? It's harrowing,"
my boyfriend asked, as I sat through a marathon
of a show about defying death.
This from the man whose favorite film
was by Rob Zombie,
and featured a psychopath wearing
another man's face as a mask,
this from the man I left for you.

That's a lie.
I left him for your cat, your MoMA
membership, the basil you grew in your backyard.
I left him for the way you chased me
down the street after we kissed,
when I fled the party like a princess
who had to get home before midnight
or she would turn into a slut.
For the Mayakovsky quote you sent at 2am,
What will it be? Love or no-love?
You tell me.

I think back to all those hours of TV,
(*how can you watch this?*)
and pretend we have a chance,

remembering that no matter
how hopeless things seemed
for the people suffering for their
bad decisions, misread maps,
there was always something
to save them in the end.
But life isn't a Meg Ryan movie,
women don't get rewarded for leaving
men they love for ones they've barely met.
When I try to see our future
all I can think of are the events
that come before the helicopters,
rescue boats, how things always get worse
before they get worse.

A couple is stranded in the ocean
twenty miles out, skin cells swollen, bursting
like roe, bodies thrashed by jellyfish.
They swim for hours, hot muscles straining,
until the shore is finally in sight.
But their relief fades fast as they realize,
they're trailing blood, attracting sharks,
and the island in the distance
is made of sheer rocks, which the waves
will crush them against.

EXIT THE VOID

"I don't want to give you relationship advice,
but you should trust people more,"
he said after dumping me
for his yoga teacher.

I'd seen this coming.
For my birthday he took me
to a three hour movie
that featured a close up
of an aborted fetus in a Petri dish.
It was romantic. The fetus
looked like a J. Crew model,
and halfway through it fell in love
with its boss at the fashion magazine
who decided they should be together
even though he had a girlfriend.

I'm kidding.
The fetus looked like a fetus.
It did not fall in love.
It did not do anything, but lie
in a pool of congealed blood.

Two months before, I had a boyfriend,
someone who carried me up the stairs
when I broke my foot,
smelled my clothes when I was gone,
tried to believe me
when I said I wouldn't leave,

begged me not to when I did
for someone we both knew wouldn't last.

After the scene, I felt like I had been assaulted,
like someone had run their fingernails
over the bloody plum of my heart,
peeled back the skin.
"Comfort me," I said.
"I am," he kissed my cheek.
I stared at the gory mass
on the screen and wondered
Where can it go from here?

SHELF LIFE

Don't worry, when I tell you
what I want from you I am not
trying to change you
I am trying to make you leave.

You were going to take me
to the Hamptons and fuck me
near the beach, but not on it
because you didn't want me to get sand
in my vagina. You were so thoughtful then.
What happened?

I'll tell you what happened:
We passed the two week mark, you
let yourself go. We ate muesli
for dinner, went to bed at 10.
You concerned yourself
with my calcium intake.

No, I do not want to have a threesome.
Or I do, but only with another woman,
and only if she is less attractive than me.

Let's do mushrooms.
Then maybe when you say
you liked me better before we met
I will not get offended.
I will say "Thank you for your
honesty. That is good to know."

Then, "What can I do
to get us back there? What
can I do to make this right?"

BURLESQUE SELF-ESTEEM WORKSHOP

I used to be homeless, but then I
joined Cirque du Soleil.

Things are better now.
I make martinis in my cleavage,
let my poodle use my stomach
as a trampoline.

I know: Let's write down our most hated
body parts, put them in a bag,
tell each other we're beautiful.

Your hair is beautiful.
Your hips are beautiful.
Your thighs are beautiful.

What I mean is: Let's walk down a runway
naked except for a clown nose and high heels.

Don't you feel better?

Close your eyes and repeat after me:
I'm healthy, I'm healthy.

LACRYMA CHRISTI

Three months in I started eating meat: sausage,
bacon, prosciutto thin as parchment. I cared
more about you liking me
than I did about the pig.

"I can't feed myself when you're gone," I said.
You laughed, but that night for dinner
I'd had an ear of corn and a bag of Caesar salad.

Most nights I'd rather drink than cook.
Lacryma Christi, the wine you ordered
on our second date, "It's all minerals, no fruit."

I just remember where it came from,
Mount Vesuvius, Tears of Christ. I sat
cross from you, my stomach full of flesh
drinking the ashes of the dead.

D FLAT IS ALWAYS TRYING TO RESOLVE ITSELF

My tooth fell out during dinner again.
I'm keeping it in a jar on my desk.
I'm sorry, this kind of thing
is always happening to me.

Remember when I was happy?
Before I stabbed the couch,
and starting spending nights at home
taking tepid baths and drinking Spanish wine
because you said it was the best I could afford?

I don't. All I remember is when
you wished I could have everything I wanted.

I wish that I wanted a room with orange walls
and a brain-damaged cat. I wish
that you wanted an anti-social stripper
who hates her day job.

Yesterday I got high and listened
to a story on NPR about tinnitus.
The worst thing about the ringing, the afflicted
man said, was that the notes in his ears were at odds.
D flat on the left always tried to resolve itself with C on the right.

I don't know about resolution,
but this hole in my mouth
isn't getting any smaller.

WE ARE NOT PILGRIMS

"You should read a book about Pilgrims," you said.
"Think about the Native Americans, all they went through."

You're right. My life isn't so bad.
I went to the dentist today for the first time
in seven years. No cavities and I don't floss.
So what if everyone I know is on a ventilator?

I will look at the bright side until I go blind.
Stare straight into the center of it like a madman
until I forget about the inside
of water globes and Siamese cats,
salt cellars and radishes.

I have a strategy for times like these:
Keep your head to the ground.
Find a face-up penny.
Canadian ones count too.

I could use a lot of luck right now.

WORD PROBLEMS

"I'm a numbers man," my uncle said when
the doctor revealed that his sister,
my mother,
had a one percent chance of surviving,
her lungs scarred and hardened, the tender
pink walls an impermeable meat.
"One out of one hundred isn't so bad."

He knew this
because he was a physicist.

"She's suffering,"
the doctors said, pointing
to the dozen thick tubes piercing
her stomach, limbs, throat,
explaining how bright
beams of pain
can break through the densest
cloud cover of drugs

What were the odds that he would
have to make this decision?
About whether to bet it all
on a losing hand,
pretend that this woman,
her collapsed body inflated
by machines, her face
an uncooked dough,
would somehow awaken,

become human again,
a princess released from a spell?

This was mine,
her only child, next of kin,
the one she left years ago
when she realized she couldn't
take care of herself or a kid.

I stood by her bed
and counted the times her chest rose and fell,
remembering how it felt
to say goodbye to someone
who was already gone.

LUNCH BREAK

If you have never cried while listening
to "Time After Time," in a deli,
waiting to buy a can of chili,
I don't want to talk to you.

I had that fantasy today where
the elderly woman standing in front
of me said I could go ahead of her
in line and when I refused, she held me.

I am constantly trying to buy you things:
over-priced chocolate, Thai basil, that book
about what to do when your girlfriend forgets
how to ride the subway alone.

As if any of it makes up for this.
As if there were no more to do
than open my arms and say here, here.

KENNEBUNKPORT

That time I bought a cocktail ring
at a flea market in Maine,
you panicked, afraid people would think
we were engaged.

We were engaged.
You proposed outside the haunted corn maze
among the hidden colonies of mice
and chinch bugs, the ghosts of pilgrims past.
Did you forget?

We drank all day, serial killed
five lobsters by freezing them
then plunging knives between their eyes,
drove for hours past farm stands, fields,
gawking at trees
like assholes who never left the city.

This was before the trips to Philadelphia,
the hours you spent in hospital waiting rooms
watching disaster movies on cable
about meteors hitting Manhattan,
and roving packs of wolves
laying claim to the abandoned public libraries.
Before I stood down the hall
and watched another world end with a sputter,
mechanical messengers
announcing it with a chorus
of beeps and gasps, stammers and silence.

Maybe we knew then, that was the best it would get.
Both of us waking each day to the sunrise,
me sitting up in the night
listening for sounds outside the house.

EARLY SPRING

What is it about someone you love dying
that makes you want to turn into a slut?

I don't know, but I do
know it's only March and it's never
felt more like spring.

When I'm not thinking about my dead
loved one, all I can think about
is fucking someone I don't love.

I've done this before.
I know how I would feel.
But I'm not interested in woulds anymore
my days are all about coulds and this
person I don't love
could feel the fat curves of my body
under theirs, the angry protrusions of bones.
They could tie me up by my child-sized
wrists, and make me forget the difference
between what they're doing
and what I want.

Then, they could lie down
pull my fragile figure close
and tell me how they will protect me
their darling damaged one
and kiss me with a tenderness
almost like a mother's.

BELTANE

Today the barrier between
the living and the dead
is as delicate as skin.

This is the light time,
the beginning of spring
when crops are harvested
and animals are sent to pasture
instead of slaughtered.

That must be why I'm optimistic,
making generous predictions about
the sick and how long they'll be around.

Nothing happens in a week.
Nettles come into season.
More friends move away.
It takes longer than that
to kill a human being.

GRAPHOLOGY

I went through a trunk of your old cards
last week in an effort to prod
the open wound of my memory,
my hands like a tongue
absently seeking out the raw pulp
of a shattered tooth.
Even then, I couldn't read them,
just stare at your handwriting.

I know what they say, the fat,
loping letters suggesting
the girlish brightness of a note
from a pen pal, or a childless aunt
instead of a mother I never talked to.
After the personality breakdowns
of your half dozen cats, the complaints about
your heating bill, comes the obvious admission
that you've been thinking about me –
I should call,
I should write.

Well I can't now,
but whose fault is that?

Yesterday I received a box of Christmas presents
that were returned to you, unclaimed by me
and re-sent by your sister after you died.
A dozen small packages wrapped
in red foil, patterned tissue
tied with ribbons run-through with wire.

I unwrapped them in my apartment
windows open to the spring,
and made myself read the tiny notes attached:
"Dear Sarah," said one,
"I hope this keeps you warm."

THE OTHER KATHERINE

When my mother died
my father asked if I thought
she should be buried next to my sister.

My sister was named Katherine,
after my mother.
She died years before
I was born.

She was stillborn.

Or not.

She emerged blue-bodied and gasping
like a fish washed ashore,
only to perish weeks later,
dried bean of a heart giving out.

My family didn't talk
about the details.

What I do know:
After Katherine died, my mother
tried to kill herself.

I don't blame her,
even knowing her success
would have come at my expense.
How can anyone be expected

to live through
their own death?
After all, those were her cells
that stopped dividing,
her veins turned to
ephemeral streams.

We buried my mother
in Pennsylvania where she died,
miles away
from my sister in Virginia.
There was no point
in keeping them together now,
both of them
so far beneath the earth,
only bodies.

TAKING PILLS IN PUBLIC

I hate to ruin your childhood,
but slice and bake cookies aren't any good.
The oil coats your tongue, forms a seal
that only the taste of sugar and preservatives can penetrate.
I'll get back to you on Hamburger Helper
when I remember how to shop for more than one thing.

All of my apertures are open.
On the best days they let in too much light,
on the worst the background blurs.
I thought slice and bake cookies
would resolve this.

You wonder why I'd do this now
when all I have at home are Whole Foods bags
filled with pictures of the dead
and imaginary places
like girl scout camp and San Francisco.

I'll tell you.
One night when you were gone
I took out my mother's coral necklace
wrapped it tight around my neck
and tried to breathe.

THE THEORY OF EVERYTHING

I'm sober all the time now.
Without drugs, I don't know
how to feel about this.

When I say that it's okay for you
to leave me here,
what I really mean is,
nothing will ever be okay again
so what's the difference?

If tragedy strikes
don't wait for flowers,
cards of condolence.
Take all the comfort you can
from useless things:
antique ink wells,
platters with grooves
for a dozen deviled eggs,
brass ashtrays with handles.

Because someday
this will all be different.
Someday we will live in a loft
on Greene Street,
own purebred cats
that are named after exotic fruit
and eat only raw foods
to treat their defective hearts.

GOLDILOCKS ZONE

My homestar has an atmosphere
of cigarette smoke and strong perfume,
Kools and Ralph Lauren.

When I was a child,
my mother let me put on her lipstick
in the car before school,
served us dinner on her wedding china
then disappeared for days.

What universal order places certain planets
at a life-sustaining distance
from their sun?
While others blaze in their proximity,
or frost over due to darkness?

When a sun dies it leaves behind
a dense mass of thermal energy,
a luminous remnant
of what it once was.
When a person dies, they leave behind
silver jewelry, paperweights.

CRICKET CAGE

Have you ever Googled yourself
and found your mother's obituary?

Don't panic.
Take your sharpest paring knife;
peel the firm, red rind of your hip,
slice open your calf and remove
the wet muscle, like popping
an edamame bean from its pod.

We went through her things
in a storage unit outside of Philly,
broken ornaments, pans with food
still stuck to them, a journal radioactive
with despair.

"You can use this for entertaining!"
her sister said, holding up a fondue kit.

I don't even entertain myself.

I took the cricket cage,
a hinged metal box meant to hold
the symbol of good fortune.

I pictured it sitting on her dresser,
way back in a time
when we believed in something
so stupid as luck.

ONE YEAR

Long story short:
everyone died.

Long story long:
everyone died and
I broke up with my boyfriend.

One year later:
the punishing brightness
drains from things
and you miss it like
a bruise,
the stormy blossom,
reminder of a pain
you don't want to fade.

Is it too late to get
an epidural?
Or are those only
for births?

These days, I hear
fire trucks and think
my apartment is burning.

HERE WE ARE

I never thought that falling asleep
would feel like dying
but here we are.

I don't know what death feels like, but I
have watched someone die
and I can't imagine it's that different.

Die, die, die

It's barely a word anymore, just a sound
like my smoke alarm that goes off
for no reason.

When my father dies he wants his ashes
shot out of a cannon like Hunter S. Thompson.

Don't get concerned if I spend
my nights curled up like a hamster
dreaming of dead relatives.
If I get upset, smother me
with your body,
your whole hard self
until I wake up gasping.

If you get upset I will peel
off my fingerprints,
and hand them to you
one by one
like tiny wings.

HONEST MISTAKE

I would have worn a mask
and fucked you
in front of a stranger,
but you got the date wrong
and we had to cancel.

You say you know disappointment
like the knots in your hand,
like the muscles in your stomach,
like the pictures of fish you draw at
night using a pen to bloat their bodies,
grant them phosphorescent lights
to make way through alien darkness.

Well, I'm sorry.
I forgot to tell you about mistakes
and how you're not allowed
to make them.
Only certain molecules
could survive all this.

BATTLE HYMN

I am overwhelmed by anniversaries,
suitcases full of jewelry hidden
in closets so they don't get stolen
or turn into ghosts.

Everything would be easier
if I didn't need food.
I could survive on painkillers
and hard candies from the bank.

You endure my unhelpful need
to be helpful
as if I could alter biology,
the painful science
of something small and sharp
moving through something smaller, tender.

While you write stories about movies
that were never made,
I watch Civil War documentaries
and have dreams about
going off to battle,
preparing to say goodbye
to everyone I've ever loved.

I'M GONNA MAKE YOU LOVE ME

There are things you don't say
to someone you're in a relationship with.
I don't know what they are
so I'm always apologizing for accidentally
being a horrible person.

I promise, I will gain back
all the weight I lost when I was sad,
then lose it again if you don't like it.
We can spend all night
in the emergency room with the drunks
who couldn't make it home,
and I'll stare at the floor for hours
trying not to be the kind of girl
who says she hates hospitals.

I will do a glove peel
with my ass crack.
Dress up like a Disney
princess and strip naked in a bar
to a song called "Gypsy Wine."

Instead of taking vows,
we can exchange ring
fingers at the first knuckle,
bitten through the bone.
Bodies shaking with anticipation
we'll extend our hands to one another
eyes closed, mouths open, like children

at their first communion,
waiting to receive the host.

ASTRO ADVICE

I don't know if it's possible to live
off Costco cookies and grocery store sushi,
but I'm willing to die trying.

Being a grown-up means
using your tax refund to buy stuffed animals,
and the perfume you wore in high school.
Being best friends means
liking the same drugs.

Adopt a scorched earth policy
with those you once loved.
Sow your heart with salt when they retreat.
Go blonde, fuck it.
What can you afford to do?

ALL MY LOVE POEMS ARE APOLOGIES

We were watching *Harry Potter*
and I had to ruin it
by talking about the future.
I'm sorry.
I didn't realize that *Harry Potter*
was supposed to be the future.

I want to home-invade your heart.
Pretend I've been stranded
by the side of the road
then force my way inside
your deepest chambers.

I wish that everything
that caused you pain
could be surgically removable.
I'd staunch your wounds
with my tongue, lick
the blood from the back
of your throat, clotted thick as jam.

You asked me why I loved
the ocean once.
I said because
you can kill yourself
just by walking into it.

COSMOS 3

There's something timeless
about this place.
A ghost preserved by light.

It's a misconception
that black holes swallow
everything that surrounds them.
Getting pulled in
means you were already
too close.

One day,
we can bring the past
to us, dance
with invisible partners.

We are at the very edge
of space and time,
where the stars
have shriveled into something
even smaller
than this darkness.

CANDLE SPELL TO ATTRACT NEW LOVE

Light a white candle
that will extinguish on its own,
then prepare an altar
of things precious to you.
Take half a Vicodin
and drink the Irish whiskey
left behind by your old love,
the one you're trying
to forget
by attracting someone new.

Do your laundry.
When you find the socks
you bought the man that left,
stuff them with
unpaid medical bills,
set them on fire
with the matches
you used to light
the candle.

Remember when he told you
he thought that making you happy
would make him want to stay.
Remember how you
are never happy.

Die,
then resurrect yourself
because you have to
go to work tomorrow.
Write your name in wax
using the thorn from a red rose.
Wait for the next full moon
and the next one
and the next one.

SLOW ON THE CURVES

People this beautiful
will either die young or never.

I stopped driving
ten years ago because I didn't want
anyone to die.
I kept hitting parked cars
and thinking someday
they'd be humans.

Everyone has promised to teach me
how to ride a bike.
Only one man actually tried.
I got angry with him
because I kept falling.
He left, but I still
have his shoes.

HAPPY BIRTHDAY

When we met, you said
you wanted a woman
who could kill you.
I forgot about this,
and kept trying to keep you alive.

Last year, I bought you a winter coat
grey, with anchors on the buttons,
extra lining, the kind of thing
someone else would wear,
a person concerned
with enduring the cold.

This year, I planned to get you
the Dune board game,
and the ability to keep your blood
in your body.

I would tell you "Happy Birthday,"
but speaking to you
when we're apart
makes me feel like my skin
is separating from my bones.

Instead, I will dance
with a stranger
eat vegetables with dinner,
attempt to give you the gift of moving on.

MAKING DINNER FOR SOMEONE ELSE

I cooked for you even when
you couldn't eat.
When your body
kept breaking open
and trying to kill you,
I made a sludge
out of lentils and spinach
that was supposed to thicken
your blood,
prove my devotion.

Salmon *en papillote*,
chicken *cacciatore*,
Brussels sprouts with black rice.

Now that I'm alone, I
smoke Parliaments,
drink 7–11 coffee, call
it lunch.
Buying real groceries
creates a dumb ache,
in a heart that's so ripe
for your love
it feels rotted.

When a friend comes over,
I make lamb ragu with ricotta,
aware I have nothing to lose.
This could be the best

meal of their life,
and at the end of the night,
I already know
they will leave.

THE VELVET SEASON

My wounds
have been so salted
they're cured.

There are things I cannot
think about:
Austin, Texas
All of Texas
Neckties and Top hats
Cockroaches and Tardigrades
Moscow
The Moon

When you're gone
I fill out online surveys
for people who are trying
to steal my identity,
lie awake and fantasize
about carving my name
into my thighs with
a kitchen knife.

My heart is a wad
of wet paper towels,
a raw steak, a bath toy.

I'm tired of pursuing
troubled people.
They should be
pursuing me.

NIGHT AT THE MÜTTER MUSEUM

My boyfriend had just left me,
and my father was still alive,
though not for long.

My father.
This is how well he knew me:
For Christmas, he got me
a chocolate bar
with Andy Warhol's picture on the wrapper,
a stuffed cat wearing a Santa hat,
and a copy of *The Semi-Homemade Cookbook* by Sandra Lee.
I read the most repulsive recipes to him,
while he read to me from a copy
of *Garden & Gun* magazine
that he had bought for me
to give to him
because he thought it would be funny.

The next day we went
to the Mütter Museum in Philadelphia.
Since my break up, my heart felt raw
and bloody enough to be wrapped up
in butcher's paper,
I was at home among
the exposed vital organs, bones laid bare,
cabinets filled with deformed
fetuses in jars.
I knew what it felt like to be
pickled, preserved,

told that there's a future out there
and maybe you're in it,
maybe you're not.
It occurred to me that having
a conjoined twin might be worse
than being lonely.

Looking back, it seems fitting
that this would be our last day together,
not knowing that soon my father's body
would be reduced to this same
collection of parts.
We spent all afternoon touring these vestiges
of death and disease
making ourselves comfortable.

OCEAN OF STORMS

It's melodramatic to say you're an orphan
when you're an adult.
Yes, my parents are dead,
but it's not like I became
a ward of the state.

I take pills to save
my shedding hair,
to fill the holes
in my dissolving bones,
to speed my heart,
and make it ache
from something other than grief.
I tease my ex-boyfriend
by threatening to leave him
things in my will.
He accepts my cat,
refuses my books.

I spend my father's money
on things that will make me
too beautiful to die, or at least
too beautiful to care
that everyone else already did:
expensive red lipstick,
a dress covered in birds
flying toward nothing.

RETURN TO OZ

I called because I needed you
but also because
you're one of the last people I love
who is still alive.

We've been here before.
We sat in diners,
ate grilled cheese and apple pie,
stood alone
in empty rooms surrounded
by the sound of chanting monks.

This time there are rules.

If you're wandering
through the desert
don't fall down,
or your body will turn into sand
then scatter
in the parched wind.
If I kiss your face,
my head will be removed
and placed in a glass cabinet
with all the other mouths
that have made the same mistake.

I cried when I realized
this was a ghost love,
the spirit of our past returned

from the dead
to hold my hand, haunt my heart.

"Think about sadder things," you said to comfort me.

BFF

Saying you have a best friend
feels childish until
most of your family dies
and it starts to mean
twin, soothsayer, lifeguard.
Two years ago my mother died,
then my grandmother.
This time it's my father.
When Leigh comes over
I am sitting on the couch
burrowed in a hamster nest
of tissues and stained quilts.
My hair is in a ponytail
on top of my head and she tells me
I look like a Barbie doll.
"That's me," I say
"Seen Too Much Barbie!"
I am hilarious
when I'm traumatized.

She brings me a stack of
Glamour magazines
and a copy of *Survival at Auschwitz*.
I only want to read about
beauty tips and genocide.

We drink cheap wine, make plans
for the future
that include a trip to Paris

and her parents
adopting me.
Occasionally I stop our conversation,
say I have to cry.
It's like throwing up,
violent and emptying.

"I don't understand
how this happened," I say
over and over again
until it no longer makes sense.
None of this makes sense.
The people who brought me
into the world are gone
and if I am them and they
no longer exist,
what does that make me?

Eventually she has to leave.
It's late, the bottle's empty.
We hug and say goodbye,
both of us buzzing, red-cheeked,
so alive.

SEA OF CRISES

I've kept the funeral
flowers so long
they're as dead as my father,
wilted to dust.

When people ask me
what they can do,
I say, "You're doing it.
Call. Listen."

What I want to say is,
"Send presents."
Gold glitter eyeliner,
a confetti cake
with frosting so sweet
it melts my teeth.
I open sympathy cards
and wait for checks
to fall out.

I have a drawer full
of pills given to me
by loved ones,
a closet full of party dresses
that I catalogue in my head,
like saying a prayer to a future
where it will matter
if I'm sexy.

I want to find a way
to quantify despair.
I see your crippling loss
and raise you two.

I know this isn't a contest,
but I've won.

EGG BOUND

I am bored by everything
but death and romance.
I don't know what to do
with anyone who doesn't want
to kill me or fuck me.

I want to dance on
champagne legs,
fall in love with someone
I can live without.

Being this sad is an athletic endeavor,
an endurance test.

I have been bled
dry as a wasp wing,
left egg bound by grief,
giving birth to shells.

SEA OF ISLANDS

Eventually you discover that in addition
to the tragedies you have already endured
comes the burden of other people
being terrified by the dark force
of all of your problems.
You are a beautiful, cursed charm,
a broken toy, pantyhose stuffed
ragdoll with one eye.
It is a power, to repel men
this thoroughly, to be so damaged
it's scary.

Your apartment is haunted
by artifacts from the past.
There is a collection of ashes
in your top dresser drawer,
both of your parents,
your childhood cat.

This is not romantic.
This is not a den of seduction.

"You seem closed off," they say,
over dinner at a restaurant you cannot afford.

"I am a ghost imitating a human being,"
is how you want to reply.

Instead you open up,
allowing the pierced yolk of yourself
to ooze out, cover them,
and the hurricane strength
of all of your suffering,
to carry them away.

MARIANA TRENCH

I am operating with a new range
of emotions that only exist
in the darkest reaches of the ocean,
among the eels and anglerfish.
You have seen their lights,
but I have felt their teeth.

I lie awake next to you thinking
I don't know how to do this,
until the anxiety is enough to overwhelm
my system, short-circuit it to sleep.

It does not make you a coward
to be incapable of loving me.

I once saw a pigeon with a broken wing
stumbling along the sidewalk.
I felt so much love for it, this pathetic wounded thing.
I imagined everything I could do to save it,
then cried as I walked away.
There were millions in the city,
and it must have carried parasites, diseases.
I did not want to get them on me.

RED SHIFT

The promise of any new relationship
is followed by my assurance
that I am simply collecting
more people to miss.

Everyone knows
the best way to draw someone
close, is to stop loving them.

"I feel like I'm making you sad
just by existing," said every man
I've ever met.

How do I tell them
I am filled with the dead?
That my heart is a bellows
puffing out air?
That true bonds are built
on how much of your blood
I have seen, how many bodies
you have helped me bury?

I only know one way
to tolerate the end of things:

None of this ever happened.
You don't even exist.

FULL DISCLOSURE

I'm going to be honest,
this is how I spend most Saturday nights:

I watch *The Real Housewives* alone, and for dinner
I heat up a "satisfying serving"
of frozen macaroni and cheese.

I make it in the oven because it tastes better this way,
the cheese forms a crust and browns at the edges.
Also, I do not own a microwave,
and using the oven makes me feel like I'm cooking.
I steam some broccoli because I do not want
to die from malnutrition.

Here are the other things I eat:

Reese's Peanut Butter Cups
Blocks of fancy cheese
Baguettes
Tomatoes
Barbecue potato chips
The tops of blueberry muffins

You'd think this diet would make
me heavy, but I am grief-thin.
I've started wearing crop tops just because I can,
the white slice of stomach my consolation
prize for the world blazing
into a wasteland.
I collect tiny designer dresses
like I don't have to pay my rent.

Because I know that even this
will end eventually.
I will continue living without
the people I could not
live without, and my body
will forget how to feed itself on loss.
When it does I will mourn
the time when I lost all that weight,
when I was so small, so frail,
almost nothing.

HELLRAISER

Every relationship
is a horror story,
each one, a house built on
haunted ground.

We all know it's a mistake
to raise the dead,
but who has that ever stopped?

I brought you back,
an instar, your shell split,
meat exposed,
fluids boiled down
to thick preserves,
your marrow dried to grape nuts
in your bones.

I clothed your wet nerves
in the scraps of men
I hunted for their skin,
gave you a heart
built to beat
with someone else's blood.

There's too much at stake
to believe that things
can never be the same,
despite your printless fingers
in my mouth,
your lidless eyes
an empty albumen.

SUMMER WATER

I'm not an alcoholic,
but I lie to my psychiatrist
when he asks
how much I drink.

I come from a long line of women
who luxuriate in pain,
adorn themselves in velvet trauma,
spend their days
in coffin-dark rooms using wine and longing
to summon dead loved ones.

All I want to do is play chess
with a set made from dead mice,
read books about women
who were murdered
by strangers,
take boiling baths
in dirty tubs.

In a crowded bar,
I spill whiskey on my leg
and rub it in.

31

I can deal with growing older
as long as I also grow
more glamorous.

I want to have fake
nails, fake boobs
and real furs.

There's nothing more glamorous
than smoking for your entire life
and never getting cancer.

As a child, I thought
my mother was glamorous.
She only wore silver
because she said gold looked cheap,
smoked unfiltered cigarettes ringed
with red lipstick.

The last time I saw my mother
was two years before she died.
She was haggard,
poor thin, not rich thin,
clutching a pillow to hide
a non-existent paunch.
It was like she had molted
with age, shedding her silk nightgowns,
heavy perfume
and emerging a pale callow.

Now my role models are:
Dolly Parton
Ru Paul
The beautiful murderesses on Columbo
in that order.

At a cabaret show,
I heard Justin Bond say
"It takes guts to be glamorous,"
before recounting a story about a woman
who cut her finger at a party
then bit off the dangling tip
and spit it in the toilet.

I AM RITA HAYWORTH AND
YOU ARE ORSON WELLES

On my birthday we got into a fight
because you started talking
about how great Orson Welles was and I said

But what about Rita Hayworth?
What about the way he cheated on her
when she was pregnant, then left
her because she was too insecure
even though when they met
that was the very thing
he liked most about her,
the way she was too damaged
to be seduced
by her own glamour,
because what had it ever
gotten her except a father
who pretended to be her husband
and a husband who acted like her pimp?

I guess it's unfair
to get mad at you for the failings
of the dead.
I just want to feel like there's a precedent
for our dysfunction.

When we met,
I was a burlesque dancer
and you were a genius.

Now you are a genius
and I am an orphan.

It's the truest path to heartbreak
when all you have to offer is your beauty
and your trauma
held out like a jewel
that only loses value over time.

Years from now, when
you've lost your dignity
and I've lost my mind
you'll approach me at a party
and wonder if I recognize you.

You'll grasp my hand, lie
about how beautiful I look
and when I start to cry
that's how you'll know,
I remember everything.

SEA OF COLD

Not only have I put all my eggs
in your basket,
I have incubated them,
they have hatched, and now
they're co-dependent chickens.

I have a scar on my wrist
from a man who meant nothing.
I should have gotten stitches,
but I wanted a reminder
of what happens when I get drunk
and pretend to want someone else.

You used to say you could see
an island in my eyes,
back when you still studied me
when my bedroom was a wonderland
of sweat, and glitter.

I know you are disturbed
by the ferocity of my affection.
Would it soothe you if I said
I only want you for your corpse?

US

"Sometimes I think about having kids," I said.
And you said,
"Sometimes I think about getting fish."

Sometimes I think you take showers
just to get away from me.

I am too old for this.
How many men have I wanted
more than food,
only to find years later,
that revisiting their memory
feels like sorting through a box
of someone else's old photos?

Last night I had a dream
I was pregnant
and happy about it.
That's how I knew I was asleep.

I keep picturing the life
we could have
if either of us wanted it.

ACKNOWLEDGEMENTS

I'm very grateful to the editors of the journals in which these poems originally appeared:

'So Emotional' in *Two Serious Ladies*; 'When Love Goes Wrong,' 'Lacryma Christi,' 'D Flat is Always Trying to Resolve Itself,' 'Word Problems,' 'Lunch Break,' 'Beltane,' in *Escape into Life*; 'Major Delusions' in *Bone Bouquet*; 'I Shouldn't Be Alive' in *InDigest*; 'Exit the Void,' 'Graphology,' 'The Theory of Everything' in *f:wriction review*; 'Shelf Life,' 'We Are Not Pilgrims' in *Mondo Bummer*; 'Burlesque Self-Esteem Workshop' in *Thrush*; 'Kennebunkport,' 'Taking Pills in Public' in *Sink Review*; 'Early Spring' in *Time Ghost*; 'The Other Katherine,' 'Honest Mistake' in *Public Pool*; 'Goldilocks Zone,' 'Astro Advice' in *Quaint;* 'Cricket Cage' in *NAP*; 'One Year' in *Plain Wrap*; 'Here We Are' in *The Doctor TJ Eckleburg Review*; 'Battle Hymn' in *30xLace*; 'I'm Gonna Make You Love Me' in *Plain Wrap*; 'All My Love Poems Are Apologies' in *LOVEbook/glitterMob*; 'Candle Spell to Attract New Love' in *Ghostwriters of Delphi*; 'Slow on the Curves' in *glitterMob*; 'Happy Birthday,' 'Return to Oz,' 'BFF,' 'Red Shift' in *Split Lip*; 'Making Dinner for Someone Else' in *Big Lucks*; 'The Velvet Season,' 'Sea of Crises' in *Luna Luna*; 'Ocean of Storms' in *Pouch*; 'Egg Bound,' 'Mariana Trench' in *Yes, Poetry*; 'Sea of Islands' in *Incessant Pipe*; 'Hellraiser,' 'Us' in *Fanzine;* 'Summer Water,' 'I Am Rita Hayworth And You Are Orson Welles' in *Flapperhouse*; 'Sea of Cold' in *Ampersand Review*.

A huge thank you to everyone who has supported me in one way or another in the years it took to put this collection together: My aunt Susan for having a heart the size of the world and for

showing me the importance of maintaining a sense of humor
in the face of deeply un-humorous situations.

My wonderful friends and mentors who have read my work and
offered encouragement; Rachel Lyon, Pat Hipp, Emily Cressy,
Wren Hanks, Max Bean, Molly Gandour, Ben Lasman, Wah Mohn,
Anjali Khosla, Chris Leslie-Hynan, Zach Graham, Lena Valencia,
Anne-E Wood, Jake Lipman, Rene Obstfeld, and Nat Bennett.

Everyone at Black Spring Press Group for all the hard work they've
put into publishing this collection; Todd Swift, Cate Myddleton-
Evans, Amira Ghanim, Edwin Smet, and Jane Collins. Kendra
Allenby for her beautiful cover art. And a special thanks to Lloyd
Schwartz for selecting my collection along with Ross White's
as the winner of the Sexton Poetry Prize.